Weird, wild, and wonderful

Seabirds

Gareth Stevens
Publishing

By Julie Murphy

Please visit our Web site **www.garethstevens.com**. For a free color catalog of all our high-quality books, call toll free 1-800-542-2595 or fax 1-877-542-2596.

Library of Congress Cataloging-in-Publication Data

Murphy, Julie, 1965-
 Seabirds / Julie Murphy.
      p. cm. — (Weird, wild, and wonderful)
 Includes index.
 ISBN 978-1-4339-3579-4 (library binding)
 1. Sea birds—Juvenile literature. I. Title.
 QL678.52.M87 2010
 598.177—dc22
                                 2009043882

Published in 2010 by
Gareth Stevens Publishing
111 East 14th Street, Suite 349
New York, NY 10003

© 2010 Blake Publishing

For Gareth Stevens Publishing:
Art Direction: Haley Harasymiw
Editorial Direction: Kerri O'Donnell

Designed in Australia by www.design-ed.com.au

Photography by Kathie Atkinson
Additional photographs from iStockphoto.com: Colin Ochel, p. 9a; Wouter van Caspel, p. 9b; Paul Tessier, p. 13b; Steve Engelmann, p. 14; Ai-Lan Lee, p. 18a; Igor Karon, p. 18b; Andrew Howe, p. 21.

Printed in the United States of America

CPSIA compliance information: Batch #CW10GS: For further information contact Gareth Stevens, New York, New York, at 1-800-542-2595.

Contents

Action!

Seabirds spend lots of time at sea. There are many different kinds of seabirds. They can do very different things.

Gannets fly high in the sky. Then they make a wild, head-first dive into the sea. They hit the water hard. They have special air pockets in their face and chest. These soften the blow. It's like having built-in cushions.

Penguins jump through the waves like dolphins.

Fact Bite

The largest albatross has a long **wingspan**. It is longer than the height of a basketball hoop!

A frigate bird is like a weird pirate. It pulls other birds' tail feathers in midair. It makes the birds drop their fish. Then the frigate bird dives and catches its meal.

Penguins can't fly at all. They are clumsy on land. Yet they are wonderful swimmers. Their wings act as **flippers** to "fly" underwater.

Petrels fish while flapping just above the sea. Their feet hang down. They look like they are walking on the water.

Albatrosses use ocean winds to glide far out to sea. They hardly need to flap their wings at all.

5

All Shapes and Sizes

Seabirds come in many weird shapes and sizes.

The smallest adult penguin is about as heavy as a carton of milk. The biggest adult penguin weighs about the same as a German shepherd!

Gulls

The albatross has a hook on the end of its beak.

Seabirds have beaks that suit the food they catch and eat in the wild. An albatross has a beak with a sharp hook on the end. It is perfect for snatching fish from the sea. Gulls have beaks that are less hooked. That is because they eat different foods from both land and sea.

Puffins' beaks are brightly colored in the **breeding season.** Later on, the bright cover falls off.

The Australian pelican's beak is longer than a computer keyboard. The pouch below the beak truly can hold more than its belly can!

When it is time to **breed**, adult male and female birds choose a **mate**. First, they do special **courtship behavior**. Next, they form pairs. Then they make babies.

The male booby (on the right) is giving the female a gift of dried seaweed.

These two brown boobies are courting. They touch each other's beaks.

8

Seabirds have some weird ways of attracting a mate. A male frigate bird blows up a red pouch on his neck. He can keep it puffed up for hours. It is his way of **impressing** the girls.

Crested grebes have a wonderful courtship dance. It includes beak-to-beak head quivering, diving, "walking" on water, and weed shaking. They check each other out very seriously. They also **mate** for life.

The male frigate bird is puffing up his neck pouch. He wants to attract a female.

These crested grebes are showing each other that they would be good mates.

Breeding Colonies

Seabirds return to the land when it is time to breed. They form groups called colonies. Each colony is usually in the same place every time.

A **breeding colony of king penguins** can get very crowded. There's safety in numbers.

Many seabirds breed on lonely islands and steep cliffs. These places are safer from land **predators**, such as foxes. Often, a few kinds of seabirds share a cliff ledge. Each lives on a different level, like high-rise apartments. Breeding colonies can be different sizes. They range from tens to millions of seabirds.

Thousands of gannets form one breeding colony. Each gannet fights for its own tiny space. Neighbors coming too close are pecked with a sharp beak.

A gannet breeding colony

While parents fish at sea, chicks wander through the colony. Returning parents call to find their youngsters in the crowd. They somehow pick out each others' cries from all the noise!

Battle to Arrive

A bird's egg is a wonderful thing. Its shell protects the baby growing inside. The yolk gives the chick food. Tiny holes in the shell let air pass through. The chick absorbs all the yolk. When the chick has no more room to grow, it is time to **hatch**.

Hatching is hard work. It can take days. First, the chick must break through the shell. It uses its egg tooth. Then the chick cuts right around the egg. It pushes with its shoulders and feet. At last, the shell splits in two. The chick is free!

A gull chick breaks through the shell of its egg.

At last the chick breaks free. Its feathers are damp from the fluid inside the shell.

The chick soon becomes fluffy.

Some seabirds lay their eggs on beaches. They don't build nests. Their eggs are colored and speckled to look like sand or pebbles. This helps hide them from predators.

Fact Bite

An egg tooth is a tiny knob at the end of a chick's beak. It breaks the shell during hatching. It later drops off.

The least tern lays its eggs on the beach.

Going Fishing

Seabirds have weird ways of catching fish.

Some snatch fish from the sea's surface. They don't even land on the water! If they did land, they might not get back into the air.

Petrels grab fish as they flap and "run" on top of the water. Frigate birds snatch fish as they fly. They also steal food from other seabirds in midair. Gannets dive-bomb into the sea. Then they chase fish underwater. Penguins catch fish while swimming underwater. Their wings make wonderful flippers.

Some pelicans dive-bomb when catching fish.

Fact Bite

The short-tailed shearwater can dive deeper than 230 feet (70 m). That is almost three tennis courts deep!

Table Manners

Some seabirds are **scavengers**. They eat all sorts of dead creatures they happen to find. The birds can't always find a dead animal when they are hungry, though. Most of the time they have to catch their own fish to eat. When they see a dead fish or other animal, though, they make the most of it!

These seagulls are looking for food to eat.

This albatross may be looking for a tasty dead squid to eat.

Petrels like this one will eat another dead petrel if they happen to find one.

Giant petrels might eat dead seal pups they find in seal colonies. They also eat dead whales and squid. Some albatrosses also eat dead squid. It's one of their favorite meals!

Amazing Feats

Seabirds do amazing things.

Every year, Arctic terns fly from the **Arctic** to the **Antarctic** … and back again! That's a trip of about 22,300 miles (36,000 km). Ocean winds help them go the distance. It sure is one weird way to avoid winter!

This group of pelicans is fishing as a team.

Arctic tern

Pelicans sometimes fish as a team. First, they surround a school of fish. Next, they scoop up the fish. Their beaks are like fishing nets.

The blue-footed booby lays its eggs on hot, sandy beaches. It has a wonderful way to stop its eggs from getting too hot. It stands between them and the sun. It casts a shadow over them. The shade cools them down.

A big fish means more food. But big fish are harder to gulp down. They take longer to swallow. Other birds have more of a chance to steal them. This masked booby chick is holding a feather in its beak, just as it would a fish. It seems to be practicing for when it grows up!

Fact Bite

Many seabirds visit the polar regions just for the summer. But some penguins live in the Antarctic all year round.

Housekeeping

Most seabirds don't use nests.

Guillemots lay their eggs on the ledges of steep cliffs. The egg has a pointy end. If an egg moves, it rolls in a circle. It won't fall off the ledge.

The white tern's egg is laid straight onto a tree branch! Chicks have big, clawed feet. These feet grasp their perches. They won't let go until they are ready to fly. That's five weeks later!

The emperor penguin lives in the icy Antarctic. Each dad balances his single egg on his feet. His warm tummy skin covers it. If the egg falls onto the ice, it will quickly freeze!

This masked booby stays with its chicks. It helps them stay clean. It also helps them stay hidden from predators.

This penguin stays close to its chick.

Fulmars spit sticky, wet matter from their stomachs at anyone coming too close. It smells horrible. It can make waterproof feathers leak. It can also affect birds' ability to fly. The chicks spit, too. Fulmar parents are very careful when returning home from fishing. They don't want a nasty surprise from their own kids!

A fulmar on its nest

21

Fact File: Special Seabirds

Seabirds spend lots of time at sea. There are many different kinds of seabirds. They are different shapes and sizes. They live all over the world. They find their food in different ways. They move in different ways.

Special Seabirds				
Bird	**Size**	**Where it lives**	**How it catches its food**	**Main way of moving**
penguin	medium to large	Southern **Hemisphere**	swim	swim, walk
gannet	large	most of the world	dive and chase	fly
albatross	large	far out to sea	surface snatch, dive, scavenge	glide
puffin	small to medium	Northern Hemisphere	dive, swim	walk, swim
skua	medium to large	worldwide	dive, steal, scavenge, hunt	fly
petrel	medium	far out at sea, mainly in the Southern Hemisphere	surface snatch, dive	fly, glide, dive, "walk" on water

Glossary

Antarctic having to do with the area around the South Pole

Arctic having to do with the area around the North Pole

breed to make babies

breeding colony a group of animals that are making babies

breeding season the time when animals make babies

courtship behavior how animals act when they are trying to attract a mate and breed

flippers broad, flat paddles for swimming

hatch to come out of an egg

hemisphere half of Earth

impressing drawing interest or attention

mate (a) a breeding partner

mate (to) to become partners

predators animals that hunt other animals for food

scavengers animals that find and eat dead animals

wingspan the length from one wing tip to the other

For Further Information

Books

Enticott, Jim. *Seabirds of the World*. London, UK: New Holland Publishers Ltd., 2002.

Scott, Leslie. *Sea and Coastal Birds of North America*. Toronto, Canada: Key Porter Books, 2008.

Web Sites

Annotated List of the Seabirds of the World
http://www.oceanwanderers.com/Seabird.Home.html

USGS: Seabirds
http://www.absc.usgs.gov/research/seabird_foragefish/seabirds/index.html

Publisher's note to educators and parents: Our editors have carefully reviewed these Web sites to ensure that they are suitable for students. Many Web sites change frequently, however, and we cannot guarantee that a site's future contents will continue to meet our high standards of quality and educational value. Be advised that students should be closely supervised whenever they access the Internet.

Index